I0162871

Table of Contents

Preface 2

Introduction 8

Chapter One: Fishless Fisherman 12

Chapter Two: Landing the Big One 18

Chapter Three: Hurry Up and Wait 26

Chapter Four: Fish in Hand 32

Chapter Five: You get a line 40

Chapter Six: Slimy Worms 48

Chapter Seven: Picky Fishermen 55

Chapter Eight: Where the Fish Are 62

Chapter Nine: When We Become the Bait 70

Chapter Ten: Equal Opportunity Aquatics 77

Chapter Eleven: When the Fish aren't Biting 82

Chapter Twelve: Catch and Release 89

Conclusion: Everyone Oughta Fish 95

Appendix: USA Fishing Holes

Dedication

There are few certainties in life. Some things are more probable than others. Still, life has a way of yielding many surprises. Such thought has led to this dedication. I may write a number of books in my lifetime. Then again…this might be it.

I will leverage this moment as if the latter might dictate.

To my parents: Thank you for never giving up on me. Thank you for the independent spirit you formed within me. Thank you for multiple chances in life.

To my wife: Please see the section entitled "To my parents". Just kidding.

Thank you for loving and believing in me. Thank you for enduring numerous difficult years in ministry. Thank you for the Christ-follower example you are to our children. I love you.

To my kids: I love you and am proud of you. To quote your grandfather, "Go do your thing".

To my church family: We've come a long way in 10 years. It makes me wonder what God has in store over the next decade. I couldn't be more proud of Hope The Breakfast Church. You're trend setters.

To Lawrence Chewning, Keith Stephens, Tom Paino Jr., Johnny Garrison, Tom Rakoczy, John Samples, and the board of HTBC: You provided me accessible examples of what it means to live for Christ as well as opportunities to be involved in ministry. I will be forever grateful.

I hope you find the material contained herein motivational and thought provoking. If you read something that offends you in any way…it's your fault. You made me this way.

PREFACE

Who is this book for?

My wife asked me that after I had written the first 20 pages. I don't think I responded defensively, but the question was a bit of a surprise, the timing of the inquiry catching me just a bit off guard. I recall answering the question by telling her what the book wasn't going to be, avoiding the question directly since no immediate answer was available. It wasn't going to be a text book. My exact words to her, "I gave up on being deep long ago". I'm not wired that way. I loved the college campus during my college years…which I did my dead level best to extend as long as possible. I like to tell people I took the scenic route in getting my degree. Still, my love for all things collegiate is not sufficient reason to compose a text book. I'm not sure American Christiandom needs another text book anyway.

Nor am I much of a touchy, feely guy. My family expressed love with a pat on the back and a $20 bill. That might sound cold to the huggers among us, but they don't take hugs at the gas station…and they don't take American Express. Because I'm not that guy with a soft shoulder to cry on, I doubt that many women will want to read my material, and since that leaves only men…and a lot of guys I know don't read…well, this book may be in trouble from the very start.

So it's not a touchy, feely text book sort of thing. It contains no deep insights, secret keys to success, or details any sort of three-step process toward life change. I believe you'll find more questions than answers, that focus on questions being purely intentional. As American Christians, I'm not convinced that we're all that good at following Christ in the obvious, much less drilling into the gray or obscure. One could make a case for our obsession with all things "deep" as an excuse to avoid personal evaluation primarily on the basis of obedience.

Have I mentioned that I'm a pastor?

I've had the privilege…and I don't use that word flippantly…to serve in full-time ministry for 27 years. My only reason for noting such is that I've heard numerous times over the years of a need for deeper teaching. My goal is not to drill deep for the sake of impression. I'm not overly concerned with balance. I wonder if our continual pursuit of balance has not yielded us mediocre on both sides of the equation. My goal is to ask just enough questions or provide just enough irritants that you and I are moved off of center and gain momentum in some direction. I'm either faith-filled or lazy enough to leave the direction that we move up to the Holy Spirit.

I guess you could say the target of this book, the vast reading audience which has filtered the material and justified the milling of at least one tree, is composed of….me. In many ways, I'm writing this book for myself.

That may seem incredibly selfish, but let me propose how it might be equally beneficial.

I think I took one psychology class in college. I couldn't give you the technical terms or dissect the reasoning behind the philosophy I'm about to expose to you…but thus far in my life, it's worked out pretty well.

I believe the people who have real influence on our lives are the people in which the moment we look into their eyes, we see a little bit of ourselves in return, or at a very minimum…the person that we long to be. That need not be much…some of the people who have influenced my life are far different from me…but in every case, and to varying degrees…I believe they have all believed in me. Furthermore, they all possessed something that I believed was a personal, potential possession.

Say that three times fast.

If I chose to live my life the way in which they lived theirs, I could have the same potential outcome. Just typing that statement brings a sense of awe. At 53 years old, are there young people in my life that would say the same things about me? Would those kids share the same last name as I? There's a thought that just might prevent a good night's rest.

The people that have had greatest impact on me are those that related to a portion of my life, saw value in fellowship, and were willing to invest as well as sacrifice time.

I recently received a compliment that meant more to me than the person paying that compliment could ever know. He stood in the doorway of my office and proclaimed, "I told my barber…our pastor could be standing in the middle of a crowded room, and you'd never know it…that's because he's one of us." I took "one of us" as an indication of the two way street which defines relationship. Iron sharpening iron as defined in scripture.

Such is what I had in mind when I sat on my back porch in the cool of the evening and began composing these words for…us. If you're a Christian or a follower of Christ (sometimes those are two completely different folks…but we'll get into that later), then this book is for…us. Sometimes I am a Christian…other times I've been a true follower of Christ, that make sense?

If you've got questions about God and His ability to speak into your life, then I hope you'll find this book thought provoking. If you're frustrated with the attitude of the church in America, then hold on….I am too. We'll have a whole lot of fun getting frustrated together. Maybe we'll work through that frustration, admit our weakness, seek God and discover a movement of unashamed believers willing to once again be freaks for Jesus.

I wrote this book for people like me, and I believe I'm a really normal guy. As normal as a 53 year old, white guy with a wife of 26 years, three kids, two dogs, a SUV and a 30 year mortgage can be. I wrote this book for a generation of people who have heard of God's exploits in the church in days of old…but have yet to see like manifestation without manipulation.

This book is for people who refuse to play the game any longer. Who question society…both secular and religious…and wonder what foundation we are building our lives upon and the impact, or lack thereof, on our children. It's for people who have more questions than answers…and believe a few things about the questions they have. First, those questions are worth asking. Second, there are answers to those questions. Third, serious implications are realized when such questions go unasked. This book is for people who refuse to allocate to the intellectual limbo so often labeled "tolerance" and instead believe that truth exists regardless of personal opinion or difficulty in discovering it.

Boy…you can see for miles up here on this soapbox…

Reviewing my words, this is no little undertaking, but my mom always said I had a knack for making work harder.

So let me encourage you. Go make yourself a really good cup of coffee…splurge a little…use the whole milk instead of skim. Find a good place to read and enjoy the journey. Should a question catch your attention, lay hold of it, chew on it, discuss it with friends. I believe there will be a more than one moment in the text of this book that the Spirit of God will prompt your mind and ask you to contemplate a thought or question. I encourage you to park there. No need to hurry through the material.

It would be beneficial to push aside those pre-conceived ideas…let go of history. Let's leave our baggage at the door and instead, dig through God's word and discover for ourselves what He has to say about this fishing excursion.

Together, I believe we will learn a thing or two. We should improve in our efforts by the lake. Our confidence as fishermen should grow. Above all, I hope we can enjoy a grin along the way.

INTRO

I Don't Fish

That might strike you odd…a book about fishing from a guy who admits in the opening paragraph that he largely avoids the past time. My father-in-law fishes…and he catches fish. I, on the other hand, hold a line in the water attached to a stick. Actually it's a rod and reel that I bought at our local 24 hour mega store…its red and chrome and I thought it looked rather cool.

The thrill of my last outing consisted of trying to see just how far I could cast. "Good cast" my 11 year old would say. I nod confidently toward his direction with the satisfaction of knowing I had passed my casting technique on to the next generation.

Still no fish…ah, but quite a fine cast. Just look how far out that bobber is…

I come from a long line of non-fisherman. I don't remember my dad ever landing anything of consequence nor my grandfather. I remember fishing trips. I remember the tackle box…boats and canoes…even cabin rentals close to the water enabling us to embark at just the opportune time.

But no fish.

Actually, now that I think about it, I do remember catching something on a fishing trip to Long Lake, Wisconsin…or "Lake Obvious" if you will. A gnarly looking fish of which no one could identify and seemingly everyone was afraid to touch. I remember it being thin and kind of old looking, nothing that anyone would want to stuff and put above the fireplace. A fish that kind of looked like it had given up on fish life.

If memory serves, I believe it had teeth…and was in need of some serious dental work.

With all of that said, I can't decide what's more odd. Me writing a book about fishing or you reading one that I've wrote.

It is my very inability to catch fish that inspired this book. While I've given up on catching anything aquatic other than that which accompanies hush puppies at Red Lobster, I have not given up on Jesus invitation to the disciples, "Come follow me and I will make you a fisher of men".

What exactly does that mean? I've heard it most of my life, but have rarely seen anyone fishing for people beyond the casual cast of a line. When Jesus called his fisherman disciples he chose men who were fishing for their livelihood. He chose men who lived with the uncertainty of the catch and who most certainly were troubled when the nets came up empty. It would seem that we, as Christians in

America, are more than satisfied with an occasional, recreational nibble without the effort required to reel in the big one.

Those words are not easy for me to write. Truth be told, I feel like a bit of a hypocrite writing such a book. Driving down the highway just last week my eldest child asked me a question from the back of the SUV, "How many people have you led to Christ, Dad?"

My thought…would that be in the ministry, or outside of it? Does an altar call count? What about those folks who raise a hand or fill out a card indicating their profession of Christ only to be never seen or heard from again? I actually went back to my childhood to think of telling my best friend Brian about Jesus and saying a prayer with him. But where were the adults I had personally led to Christ?

Were all of my fish friends in the same aquarium with me…the one we call the church? Did I, as a husband, father, pastor, brother, and son…really have any friends who don't know Jesus or were the unsaved people I know relegated to superficial acquaintances at best?

That's a troubling thought for me. When I consider the relationships in my life, could I classify them in following manner? Friends = Christians….Acquaintances = Non-believers

Do I have a right to cast a line in a pond of acquaintances?

And there you have it. This book is my personal fishing trip. Perhaps my lack of results in fishing could be attributed to a number of reasons. I'll pose some…and you'll probably think of more. When it's all said and done, perhaps we'll be fortunate enough to catch some fish or at least have earned the right to wade into the water.

What say you get a line and I'll get a pole and we'll just see what God can do?

Chapter One **Fishless Fisherman**

Inspiration can be found in the strangest of places. It was the thought of fishing for men that led me to the Indiana Department of Natural Resources website…or perhaps it was Parks and Recreation…truth is, I don't remember. Wherever I was on the information super expressway, I came across the following quote. "Catching a Memory"

> "…these top predator fish are the product of special fishing management programs that lure-in anglers to catch these line busters. These fish are a test of your will, knowledge, and persistence. Give these waters a chance to change your life, they're already there for you."

I can almost hear the words of my childhood pastor, "Now…that will preach!"

Fish that are a test of the will, fish that require a strategic approach, and flat out require persistence in order to be successful, these, according to the website, are memory makers. Catch one of these and you'll never be the same. And the best thing of all…they're already there for you. Why not?

But there is a rub…there is a catch…literally. Seems like there always is.

Jesus said that He would teach the disciples to catch men instead of fish, but first and foremost…they had to drop what they were doing and follow Him. He would provide the lessons. He would be their teacher and they would be the students.

It would cost them their livelihood. Had these men no bills to pay? Did they not have lives at home, children to feed or at least groceries to pay for? Wouldn't the little woman be more than a little perturbed? What about the house projects, the lawn that needed aerated, the deck that required stain?

While the children of Israel received miracle after miracle from the very hand of God…and yet still fell into doubt and rebellion…it only takes one directive for Peter, Andrew, James, and John to drop what they are doing and follow a total stranger. What exactly prepared these men for such a moment? What events formed their lives and gave them the tools to make such a radical decision? Gullible…I think not. Jesus later states that it is upon Peter, a man of action and often less thought, that He will build His church. Peter may not be a master of logic, but he's not gullible. I wonder how much influence Peter had on the others as he beached the boat and refused to look behind? Has God shaped me through the circumstance of my life in such a way to make a like decision?

I have a friend who lost his wife to cancer after a five year battle. He's now raising two little boys on his own. My friend has a perspective on life that I, most likely, will never know. His journey has allowed him to prioritize what is truly important in life and, something in which I find myself a bit jealous of, has given him an intensity and urgency for decisions that must be made. I've noted how the depth of the challenges that he faced over those years have honed his faith. It seems that circumstances like his tend to break or solidify the faith of the participants. There seems to be little in between.

Perhaps requirement one in catching fish is faith. Perhaps the faith required is based primarily on remembering the past from which we've been delivered. Faith from the realization of personal transformation yields the firm belief that such is possible in the life of others. Stated another way…

It helps to believe that you're going to catch fish when you go fishing. There's nothing less motivating or more uninspiring than to wake at 4 AM in the chill of the new morning only to sit in a boat or along the shore with the absolute certainty that one is wasting their time and their efforts are futile. Why would anyone want to do that?

All of which leads me to a question I've been pondering personally and that I will pose to you. If you go down to the fishing hole every day and hold a line and pole in the water but never catch anything, are you a fisherman?

Seriously

Hang with me here for a moment. To even pose such a question brings about a certain uneasiness in my being. Not so uneasy that I won't pose the question, mind you, but uneasy nonetheless. I imagined the objections the moment I formed the thought.

"Well, of course you're a fisherman. You've got the boat, the tackle, the life vest, multiple rod and reels, the latest version of 'In Fisherman' (I just made that up). You're doing the work…you can't help it if the fish aren't biting."

I truly don't want to confuse matters, I understand the objections. I'm just doing my best not to rationalize efforts that may not be nearly as rational as we would like to think. There's a dispute as to whom gets credit for seeing God's kingdom expand in the New Testament. We're instructed that Paul planted, and Apollos watered…but it was God who brought the harvest.

Growing up in Indiana, there's not a city kid in Indianapolis whose not familiar with corn. Drive any direction in our city and within 15 minutes, you're in a corn field. In the spring they till the ground and plant the seed. The summer brings rain and in the Fall…you guessed it…they cut it all down and let it rot in the fields. After all…they're farmers.

Now come on.

Planting and watering are essential, but the objective is to get the grain into the barn…to see the grain put to productive use.

Let's position the thought just a bit differently…just for perspective sake.

a.   If you don't raise any crops…are you a farmer?

b.   If you don't produce a product, are you a manufacturer?

c.   If students never learn, are you a teacher?

d.   And for the sake of my teacher parents, if you never study, are you a student?

e.   If you don't bake, are you a baker?

f.   If you have more vacation time and perks than the working class backbone of our US of A, are you a politician?

Strike that last one.

Recently I sat in a meeting led by the president of our church denomination. I've never met a man like him, or at least a man with the attitude and perspective he embodies toward ministry.. This man shared two things that were heavy on his heart, those things of which he labeled "chilling realities". Reality one was the realization that we have people in our churches that are no longer convinced of the lostness of mankind. People no longer convinced that sin is real, or that Hell awaits those who reject Jesus as savior.

That reality certainly undermines the necessity of fishing.

He shared that reality two is that loyalty to telling people around the world that Jesus is the only way, truth, and life…something that for years we have termed "missions"…is dead. If we were unclear on the statement, he was very purposeful in saying it twice.

Financial contributions given from the well of <u>tradition and loyalty</u> is D.O.A. The new litmus test for cracking open our wallets, "does it work?"

There is a new emphasis on effectiveness. People need to know that their giving is making a difference. Or, referencing our analogy…they need to know the baker is producing baked goods. That students are passing the class, and the farmer is on his tractor bringing in a crop.

This man went on to say that such demands for impact would truly be more difficult to judge equally among all fields of the harvest, noting that some of the ground being worked is notably tougher soil than other places.

Perhaps the reason we've been content to fish with very little result has been our lack of expectation or even willingness to track effectiveness and result. Equally concerning may be the lack of life transformation and the building of faith that occurs through Spirit dependent living in the midst of trying circumstances.

Perhaps what each of us need and should desire most is to land a really big fish.

Chapter Two **Landing the Big One**

People get excited when they catch a fish   Catch a fish…and you'll return to fish again.

I've heard it said that if you play one hole of golf well, you'll return to play again. I'm only slightly better at golf than I am at fishing. Golf is a great game. For me it's a game of isolation…usually to the far right…in the other fairway to be exact. It's that element, along with the unjustifiable expense, that prevents me from seriously pursuing the game. I spend so much time on the course…not in ear shot of my co-players…but in isolation, hacking away at that little white ball…losing that little white ball…sweating without the joy of teamwork…wrestling with questions of conviction, "Did that last swing yielding a Big Mac size divot and a four foot drive really count as a stroke?"

Now that I think about it, my golf game and fishing do share a lot in common. Both involve my casting something into water…either a lure or a golf ball. Both take an increasing amount of patience, which can be a real challenge considering both are intended to be recreational, and both are absolutely voluntary in nature. No one forces me to do either…It's not like I'm making a living at these ventures. Neither activity reinforces my self-esteem and both activities involve primitive bathroom facilities, something that I have always believed barbaric and have done my best to avoid.

I guess that's why basketball is my game, always has been…always will be. But you're not holding a book on Indiana's favorite pastime. No discussion of zone vs. man-to-man defense here, we're talking fishing.

Here's my hypothesis. Just as playing well one hole of golf in an afternoon wrought with frustration will inspire a person to return and play time and again, I believe catching one fish holds the same appeal.

I've caught few in my fishing efforts…admittedly both physical fish and spiritual in nature. The few that I have had the privilege of landing we're pretty exciting and simply made me want to catch more.

They're not money fish, mind you. My eldest and I like to watch a show on Discovery called "Deadliest Catch". It's a documentary, real-life show of sorts…as real life as anything can be with a camera recording an individual's every move. Nevertheless, the camera crew is on deck to record the movements of men who fish the Bearing Sea…they face horrific weather…and chunks of ice large enough to crush the boat. They put their lives on the line for king crab…each one with a dollar sign attached to it. And when they pull a full crab pot….see, I have been paying attention….from the ocean floor…they practically do a jig.

It's all for a buck.

I've noticed myself watching with a sense of anticipation as the wench hoists that crab trap from the sea. Will it be full or is it a bust?

It reminds me of Jesus' encounter with Peter, James, and John. The story goes that they had fished all nights and were in the process of mending their nets. They probably looked a little beat up…no doubt they were exhausted. Fishing all day without catching anything had them mentally calculating bills without the luxury of income. Though they liked each other well enough…the stress of an abysmal catch had them dancing on one another's last nerve. Suffice it to say, these guys weren't in the best of moods.

Aren't you glad Jesus doesn't love us based upon the mood we're in?

Jesus looks at these worn out fisherman who had just put in a full shift and asks them to cast out to the same waters they had just fished…the same waters they had fished many times before…and fish from the opposite side of the boat. Kind of like…go on out and fish 10' to the left.

Take a moment to ponder that.

They had no idea who was making the request. It would be a little like you and I going to a construction site and asking the foreman to move the building two feet to the right. "It will work better there", you might say. Can you see the foreman's face? How long would it take for the laughter to subside before he realizes you are serious? How long does it take them to escort you to the nearest exit?

It sounds nuts doesn't it? I mean the nets have been mended…the equipment is put up…the crew has come to a mental conclusion that this just wasn't one of their more profitable days. They probably had every intention of doing every thing possible to forget the bust of a day. And now, some guy is asking them to do it all over again.

That's actually one of the things I like most about Jesus and his ministry on earth. Jesus did things that absolutely defied any sort of conventional thought, and he wasn't afraid of offending anyone by asking them to participate in the impossible. We absent mindedly call them miracles, but we fail to realize the shock that such acts caused those around him. We could spend chapter upon chapter doing our dead level best to paint a picture of the radical things Jesus asked his followers to do. Go get money for a tax payment out of a fish's mouth. Collect a few fishes and loaves and feed the masses. Deny worldly possessions, leave family and friends, pick up your cross and follow me. These are not the activities of the status quo. These are the activities of a radical.

We have the luxury of knowing the end of the story. The downside of this luxury is that it often robs from us the impact of the moment. After taking in such an incredible catch…all because these trusting fisherman went out and fished 10' to the left…these same guys forfeited the most profitable day they had ever experienced in their professions to follow Jesus.

No where does it say anything about the future disciples enticing Jesus to enter business with them. I don't believe thoughts of how they could "clean up" in the fishing industry ever crossed their minds. Upon arrival back on shore these three experienced clarity of mind and purpose unlike they had ever known before. Business was the furthest thing from their minds. Intrigue with the master fisherman ruled the moment.

Jesus didn't shock with acts alone…he shocked with words. He shocked with claims of his deity…he called out hypocrites for who they were…he stated that you and I would act with his same power and authority while simultaneously pointing all glory to him.

Now just back the fishing boat up, you say.

That's radical stuff. Jesus commanding the miracle is one thing, it's something very different when he provides his authority and Spirit to you and me. Many of us are all about the "bring the little children to me Jesus", we're just a bit confused…or scared…or intimidated to believe that the same power that flowed thru Christ is not only available today, but intended for today.

I always get a bit skiddish talking about the power of the Holy Spirit, the priesthood of the believer, and the necessity of the display of God's power in our contemporary world. My fear is that somehow people begin to confuse themselves with Jesus. Our identity is in Christ…but we are not Jesus.

Greater things than these will you do….in order that our Heavenly Father is glorified. Please don't think me sacrilegious here…but we're a little bit like a really good Elvis impersonator. We know that guy up there with the sideburns and rhinestones isn't the king…emphasis on the small "k"…but he reminds us of the real thing. Sometimes…if the light is just so and the deep vibrato of his voice is just right it's as if the Joe next door is Elvis himself.

No offense to fictional Joe…but no matter how hard Joe tries, he's never going to be Elvis. Same with you and I…no need to worry, we're never going to be Jesus. People aren't going to confuse you with the Savior. Strictly forming a logical argument, if we were capable of being Jesus, would there ever have been a need for him to die on a cross?

Still, we are called to "represent"! The very Spirit of Jesus…His Holy Spirit…desires to flow thru our very existence. He longs to empower our lives for change, to equip us for every situation, to see us mature into people that will drop everything in order to land the big one.

On second thought, perhaps it wasn't that tough for the eventual disciples to drop everything and follow Jesus. Maybe they were sick of fish, backbreaking work only to smell like carp at the end of

EVERY day. Perhaps the catch was so incredible that they simply couldn't eliminate their curiosity. Maybe they liked the idea of doing something eternal, giving their lives to something significant.

You and I have got to get to that place. I think it's pretty safe to say that in America, we're satisfied with a small catch. What fishing we've done we've relegated to the same fishing holes and the same fishing lines. Nothing new…slow, but steady we tell ourselves.

Meanwhile there's a hole in the boat. We've got to get back to a place of urgency…a sense of desperation.

I was watching that same channel the other night when a man caught a good sized salmon in Alaska and proceeded to eat it right out of the river. Never cooked it…chopped it up…or opened up a jar of tarter sauce…he just bit into that trout right then and there True, it was a survival show…and he hadn't eaten in a couple of days.

A few days later I was standing in the meat department of our grocery store and noticed a nicely shrink wrapped piece of salmon in the cooler. As God as my witness, I had no urge to rip off the plastic and take a bite. No urge. I did buy some fish sticks, but the kids and I opted to control our hunger and wait for them to be cooked.

We just weren't desperate enough. We weren't hungry enough.

Did you ever see Tom Hanks in Cast Away? That was great…really great. (in honor of Chris Farley). Tom Hanks plays a Fed-Ex employee who is stranded on a deserted island after surviving a plane crash. Hanks lost something like 30 pounds in order to play the role of a desperate, starving man. And when he finally catches a fish…and creates a fire…he has no one to share his accomplishments with.

Well, he has a volleyball, but it's a pretty one sided conversation throughout the movie…and it makes for a really tough biblical illustration. But I'll try…

Perhaps we're not as desperate to fish for men, because we…as a church and a body of believers…do a pretty poor job of celebrating the accomplishments of God. We do our best to share a witness of our lives, and we have nobody to tell. We've lost the ability to share stories of God's victories in church. We might share them on Facebook, but when it comes time to share how God has blessed our life with others…too often the request is met with silence and blank stares of confusion. That's a tremendous problem.

Perhaps we're just not hungry enough. Not desperate enough. As one person commented on my blog, perhaps we're too picky about what fish we go after. That's certainly a valid thought, and one that we'll pursue in a later chapter.

Suffice it to say, we've got a problem, a challenge, or an opportunity…depending on your disposition. We're not fishing well. We're not catching fish. And if Jesus said we would be fishers

of men, then I'm pretty sure the problem doesn't rely on him.
Perhaps we've done the wrong thing with the fish that we've
caught. Have we stuffed and mounted the few that have joined our
ranks and held on to them too tightly? Perhaps we would catch more
fish if we were more generous with their placement. Maybe it's time
to catch some fish and release others, all with the confidence that
God will fill our nets.

Chapter Three **Hurry up and wait**

Professionals don't really catch fish in 23 minutes

I've got a buddy who recently organized an effort to mobilize church attenders to perform random acts of kindness throughout the city. While I'm not big on the "random" part of the effort, my preference would be "purposeful acts", I helped in a small way as an encouragement to him.

One of the last times I saw him, he had a certain look about him. One of those "I know what we're doing is God honoring…I know it's important….but this is really, really hard work" kind of looks. You've heard the phrase "it's a little like herding cats". This was more like getting cats to do data entry.

Part of the challenge for my buddy was the American need to be productive. The people that participated that day wanted to hit the ground running…make an impact…and chalk up a win for the kingdom. Few were interested in learning more about the context in which they would be serving. A smattering more were open to instructions for the day while others simply wanted to get started with hopes of ending on time. All wanted to be effective. There's nothing wrong with wanting to be productive in our efforts, but so often you and I are so consumed with the end product that we neglect to learn from the process we engage. In our culture we want to expend minimal effort and resources while simultaneously producing a quality product with the ultimate goal of turning a profit and starting the process all over again.

That's the American way…and in many regards, I have absolutely no beef with it. If there is a something to be tweaked, I suggest the following.

In a society of pay per view, self check-out counters, and on-line everything…the problem is patience, endurance, and loyalty. As Americans, we want it all and we want it now.

The problem is that it just doesn't work that way with fishing. No matter how focused the effort might be or how many resources one might throw at the process, there is just no way to ensure a product at the end of the day. Fishing is a process of hurrying up and waiting.

I once saw an interview with a wine manufacturer…or vineyard guy…not really sure of the correct title. He stood among rows and rows of dusty bottles all laying on their side, and for some reason…which escapes me now…he would give the bottles a twist every once in a blue moon. Just a little turn…yielding a new surface on which the dust might collect. I'm talking years upon years of methodically turning bottles and letting them sit.

I don't image it's that way at the Coca-Cola plant.

But even the continual, monotonous turning of wine bottles does not compare to the challenge of waiting that you and I must endure. The wine enthusiast knows that one day his efforts will produce a vintage well worth all of the effort. And he's enthusiastic about the possibilities. Question, are we fishing enthusiasts? Are we as confident and anticipant about the eventual return from all of our efforts?

Waiting always reminds me of a scene in "The Princess Bride". The man in black is chasing three bandits who have kidnapped the princess, when the Spaniard is instructed to wait for the hero to dispose of him. Our hero struggles up the side of the cliff only to be queried by the Spaniard, "I do not suppose you could hurry up". The man in black replies, "No, I guess you'll just have to wait." To which the Spaniard replies, "I hate waiting".

I can relate.

There are times when I really hate the process of waiting. A trip to the BMV, a game of monopoly, the 30 second countdown before the next Netflix download, all are problematic. Recently, I was disappointed to discover there's a two second delay between an NFL broadcast and actual play on the field...how sick is that?

Waiting on God is a hassle. Working with little or no immediate results is overwhelming. Waiting robs my enthusiasm. I am not an enthusiastic waiter. Please don't tell me that Noah had a great attitude for 40 years while building a boat for a natural occurrence…that had never naturally occurred before. You know when I believe the biggest test of Noah's patient waiting occurred? I'm guessing every time his hammer met his thumb. Sarah laughed upon being informed that she would have a baby, knowing that she had been a card carrying AARP member for 40 plus years. Joseph waited in prison, only to be forgotten by those on the outside. The disciples found themselves in an upper room waiting on a promise of who knows what after being abandoned by Jesus. That sounds a bit rough…but I'm confident they waited in that room with a great deal of fear and uncertainty.

This chapter runs the risk of depressing the "wait-er" over lack of nibbles or bites from the "wait-ee". I hope that's not the case with you, it's certainly not my intention. What I believe you and I need to accept concerning this process of fishing, and its unavoidable component of waiting, is as follows. I hope you find it encouraging.

1. You can't make a fish take the bait. There should actually be some sense of peace that accompanies this reality. You can be wise about how you fish. You can truly take interest in the fish for which you are fishing. But no matter how hard you might try, there is no way that you can make a fish bite. Knowing that it is the Holy Spirit that does the bidding to humankind, this should make the mental stress of the fishing process a bit easier to handle.

2. Sometimes it the very last moments of the day which are the most productive. I remember one of my rare fishing adventures in which my rowboat companion caught a large mouth bass just prior to our packing up our gear and heading back to shore. We hadn't caught a thing all day long. In the last moments of the day, all the patience invested became worth the effort. Perhaps our prayers should be for the endurance to fish as well as for the catch we hope to make. What would have happened if we had packed it in just 15 minutes earlier? There's no way to know the perfect time to fish...so fish on!

3. This is a stretch...but could it be that we learn equally as much in the waiting as we do when we land the fish? When I said earlier that my friend and I spent the day in futility, having nary a bite, that description isn't entirely accurate. Tooling around the lake in that boat provided for some good conversation. We knew more about each other at the end of the day than when we began. Even the moments of silence were telling. You can learn a lot about an individual in how they respond to times of silence. Question...how long can you be silent with your friends? How long can you be silent while fishing? Silence and waiting are not passive; they're part of the process. Perhaps the lag time, the times of silence in the waiting process, is preparation for a catch that is coming your way. Knowing when to contribute to the conversation and knowing when to remain silent while actively listening would certainly make us better fishermen.

We would do well to remind ourselves that the guys on the fishing channel really don't catch all of those fish between commercials. The miracle of digital editing allows us to marvel as they reel in the catch. What they neglect to show us are the hours of endurance displayed in sitting on that bass boat with nothing to show for their efforts. That wouldn't sell much fishing equipment on commercial breaks and would make for yet another dull television program.

This, however, isn't about instant speed, trickory or miracle lures. This is about fishing and being patient in the process. So I say keep that line in the water…and fish on.

Chapter Four **Fish in Hand**

Fish are only caught when they're in the boat

I'm about to offend a number of people. I'm not offensive for any other reason than wanting to propose a topic that I believe needs to be discussed. I'm not trying to be controversial for the sake of attention. This is not an attempt to shock and awe anyone. What follows, I believe, is based on an increasing reality in our American culture. How comfortable we are with this new reality is where the controversy begins. Where it ends is only known and controlled by God. Let the discussion launch from the next statement.

Fish don't count unless you get them in the boat.

Multiple thousands of stories have been told about the one that got away…but they're told with palatable remorse accompanied with a just a hint of doubt.

In like fashion…and strictly in my opinion and observation…I believe the American church has morphed into a default mentality which accommodates "the one that got away". We're not overly concerned with reeling them in and getting the fish into the boat, unless building the attendance of the church equates reeling them in. For the most part, we're content with casting a line and holding it in the water. For instance…

How many evangelistic events (often referred to as "Outreach"…because we've grown so cynical or fearful of anything associated with Evangelicals) have we conducted in which, at the end of the day, we have little to nothing to show for it. How many concerts, carnivals, or comedians do we present in which 98% of the audience is made up of the same people you see every Sunday?

I'm not putting those people or their ministries down. If it weren't for those efforts, some of us would not be in church today. What I am trying to convey is that outreach events that no longer meet the criteria for outreach…really do not constitute outreach.

That's the part that's controversial. It's not the heart for ministry. It's not a concern for people who need Jesus. It is the simultaneous embracing of God on mission and the ineffectiveness of attraction only church wide events that places both church leaders and laity alike in an uncomfortable reality. When I understand the heart of God for every fish in the pond, then I begin to identify with the heart of God in my everyday existence, not just in the roller coasteresk adventure that so often symbolizes the ramp up preceding most outreach events only to be met by an accompanying let down once past the summit. But when I embrace God on Mission in the routine of my daily existence, I find that I develop his heart and longing for those around me. The exercise of that heart becomes a visual of the inner relationship I have with God. Evangelism moves well past a program. Evangelism simply becomes a witness of that which I've…witnessed.

I find the topic of methods of evangelism absolutely fascinating. As far as I can tell, we have spent the last 30 years making the bait more attractive and praying that the fish would come to us. We're shocked when we get a nibble…and a bit afraid when we actually land one. We've paid the clergy to act as professional fisherman, and due to our American consumer mindset, we've cast large nets known as "oversized postcards" and hoped that the portrayal of smiling faces would rouse interest.

There are, however, some blatant problems with the solitary "Come and See" approach. First, the fish we seek are growing increasingly difficult to catch. A number have taken the bait in previous generations only to discover that what was offered left a bad taste in their mouths. How many people do you know that simply aren't interested in church? I mean, it doesn't dawn on them that attending something called a service on Sunday morning could remotely impact their life. While it's true that many of our neighbors will never receive a personal invitation to church, the reason for that lack of invitation is most likely due to the number of rejections we have previously experienced. Hear "no thanks" often enough, and people have a tendency to avoid making an offer.

It's a little bit like casting a line and never getting a bite. Eventually, you pack your fishing gear and go home.

Let me propose one other possibility for the lack of invitation. Church goers aren't convinced that what they experience in a

Sunday morning setting is indeed life transformational. Again, that's one of those things that us church going folk do not like to hear. It might, however, actually be something that your friends need to hear you and I admit. The pitch-in meal isn't going to be the best food you've ever eaten. The concert won't compare with the Eagles or the Foo Fighters. The sermon won't contain the secret to the universe. Perhaps your friends, or in this case the fish in the pond, need to hear us admit that everyday life is often just everyday life for the follower of Christ. There are moments when the seas part, the multitude is fed with a sack lunch, and tongues of fire appear on the heads of the congregation, but those moments are called miracles, and miracles don't happen every day. If they did, they wouldn't be so miraculous, would they?

Here's the rub though. Instead of changing bait, fishing a different pond, or admitting that there's a new problem in our fishing adventure, the church insists that what worked in the past must continue to work in the future. Programs become sacred to the extent that changing such proves more emotionally draining and potentially detrimental than the possibility of greater effectiveness. So we keep on holding that pole and hoping for the best.

That distresses me because I'm a firm believer in the adage, "Success breeds success, failure breeds failure." I believe if we refuse to change our fishing technique, we run the risk of letting the excitement of teaching others how to fish completely escape us. Stated another way for your consideration, It's difficult for me to translate to my children how much fun it is to catch fish, when it's been a while since Dad has had that pleasure.

There is an elderly memberr in my church who knows how to fish. Almost on a weekly basis she shares with me her fishing experiences. She fishes at the beauty salon. She fishes at the big box store. She fishes with neighbors up and down her street…and she catches fish.

I do my best to tell the stories of her fishing expeditions. I keep coming back to this statement...and I'll offer it once again. We don't tell enough stories. I've delivered a ton of messages…well, maybe a couple hundred pounds of messages…but most of the time it's a good story that people will remember.

I think people place themselves inside of stories. They imagine their reactions, the emotion of the moment, the scene in which the story takes place…all while making the story their own. Isn't that what we're trying to accomplish with the speaking and teaching of God's word? The thought occurred to me the other day…if the sharing of stories, especially in light of God's word, is so important to experiencing intimacy with Christ, confidence in Him, and the ability to fish…when is it that we give ourselves to the give and take of those stories and experiences?

Let's explore the idea of story a bit further.

Could it be said that Sunday morning in America from 10:45-12:00 is one of the most non-relational moments of our weekend? It strikes me odd that people sitting on a back porch grilling out will laugh and share story after story, creating moments to remember, while people in church can sit next to each other and nary say a word.

Just as a reminder, I'm one of those guys who speaks on Sunday morning.

I'm not opposed to worshipping God thru song...personally, I love to do so. But worship is not the sum total of church.

I'm not opposed to the teaching or preaching, often differentiated merely by the number of lesson points delivered and the intonation of speech. Preparing lessons, talks, and sermons is one of the highlights of my week. But preparing and delivering the most insightful lesson is not the sum total of church.

Nor is missions, or Sunday School, hymnbooks, Powerpoint, pews or chairs...none sum up why we gather on Sunday mornings. Its possible to spend millions of dollars on a facility, gather thousands upon thousands of people, and sponsor missionaries around the world and still miss the point of church. Here's what I believe the Bible tells us about church.

You and I are the church. That big room that we meet in...the one we've referred to as a sanctuary really isn't a sanctuary for the presence of God at all. In the Old Testament, God resided on a mountain or in a temple…a place…a room. You and I see that room as a sacred place because we've equipped it with sacred imagery. The cross reminds us of his sacrifice. The stained glass tells the story of his preeminence. The pews…well, they're something that we sit on. That's not completely fair. Even the pews become sacred because they remind us of certain times when we experienced the presence of God or a milestone in life…a marriage, a funeral, baptism, or the dedication of a child. Things remind us…but we too often associate those memories with a physical object that had little to do with something significantly sacred.

We may value the mountain or the temple more than we do the radical relocation that takes place in the second half of the Bible. In the New Testament, his Spirit…the very Spirit of God himself…desires to reside in you. So as a friend of mine puts it, "In the New Testament, God puts the temple on the road."

Religious imagery? Let me suggest that we take it on the road with us. Not necessarily in physical form, but as we exit the church service on Sunday morning, how much better would we be if we took the cross with us? Can you imagine the impact that the supremacy of Christ and the story depicted in the stained glass windows of our churches would have if we filtered our daily decisions through the significance of those lessons? Do our friends see us in the individual process of building a place for God to reside, his temple, in the center of our lives or do they equate church primarily with a parking lot and a building?

The church is the church whether it's gathered on Sunday morning at 10:45 or when it's scattered at noon. When we exit the building, we do not disengage from His Spirit. There's no shifting of gear or compartmentalizing of life. You and I are the church in all its expressions and forms wherever we go.

It's that very thought…that you and I embody His Spirit…that you and I are the church…that provides a convenient segway back to the topic at hand. Since we embody the presence of God, you and I have something to share. Since we are reconciled back to the Father, we are family. Family should always have something to talk about. But it's tough to do so when there's no time for interaction…for BBQ…for a cup of coffee.

I'm not exaggerating when I say that I've been taught for over a decade that relationships are the most important key to returning the church to its missional purpose of reaching every man, woman, and child and giving them the opportunity to hear about Jesus, ultimately accepting or rejecting His forgiveness and purpose for their lives. Relationships are the vehicle most effective for such exposure and dialogue. It's about spending time…doing life with others…walking with each other in the journey of life. I've heard all of that till the proverbial cows have come home…which is a long time for the non-midwest audience. The question remains, how do we develop our relational capacity when the church has evolved into a preaching warehouse and Americans fill their schedules to the absolute brim with multiple variations of activity?

As I see it, we have two options. We can pray, hope, and believe that our American society will experience a wake-up call…suddenly seeing things our way, or we can do a bit of changing ourselves and wade into the water. Something tells me that the fish aren't going to jump in the boat.

Chapter Five **You get a line, I'll get a depth finder, honey**

Are we allowed to do anything new to reach people?

Today's writing venue is certainly different. The family has planned a vacation for some time now. Let me rephrase that...my wife planned the vacation...the kids and I are simply supposed to be in the right place at the right time. It's a well designed system. Don't mess with what works.

We saved our nickels and dimes for nearly a year in order to fulfill our ultimate obligation as good, suburban parents. We took our kids to Disney World. Saw it all in two fun-filled and thoroughly exhausting days. Today, however, represents the other extreme of all the energy that is Disney. Today I sit on a lounge chair next to the cement pond, as the Clampets were known to say, in a retirement village in central Florida.

No, I'm not THAT old...with 50 years old constituting the minimum age for buying a doublewide, technically speaking I could move in. Not certain how the retirees would feel about my kids, but it's really a moot point....not gonna happen.

The greatest generation comprises the crowd today. There are women in the pool swimming laps. I've never understood how older folks can swim so slow and stay afloat. People must become more buoyant as they age. There are a number of senior men who have waxed creative and created flotation devices out of noodles that allow them to suspend themselves vertically. Leave it to the men to eliminate physical exertion. The scene reminds me of a Bridge game without the table or cards. My favorite group of all though is the four people sitting in the hot tub. I couldn't help but overhear their conversation as they compared notes on knee surgeries.

"I'm tellin' ya…that knee cap just shifted"

"You're kidding me?"

"I swear…just shifted to the right"

They went so far as to share doctor's names…almost as if they were collecting references for future body work.

I've been invited to a church tonight to speak at the New Years Eve watchnight service. I hadn't heard the term "watchnight" for a LONG time. Reminiscent of the surroundings, the church is primarily composed of older folks. Tonight they will sing and worship God…they will pray for a new year…and they will listen to me speak.

They'll probably pray more after they hear me speak.

As I peruse the scene once more over the top of my glasses, the thought hits me. Tonight the church will pray for the fish…instead of going to the cement pond. I won't be surprised if that very thought worms its way out in my talk tonight.

My mother sits to my left. She's prayed for me all of my life. Growing up, she was on the green couch in the living room at the end of our hallway every morning reading her Bible when I walked down the hallway wiping the sleep from my eyes. She has shunned carnal things…things that are not beneficial…and lived a life focused on Jesus. But she's the first to admit that she wasn't raised to connect with sinners.

In fact, it was much the opposite. When considering scriptures instruction that we live in the world…but are not of the world…there was much more emphasis placed on the "of" rather than the "in". Be careful who you associate with, was the admonition…they'll drag you down.

I love my mom. And to her credit, she has listened to my many rants and ramblings for years. My rant today rings personal. "Mom…you're greatest ministry is not inside the walls of the church, it's next to this cement pond."

Odds are that one or two of the folks floating in the water in front of me won't be floating in the next few years. Equally as great odds are that few to none of those invited to attend church will darken the door of one. So…how do we reach them?

Pool time…kind of reminds me of "Tooltime"…but in this case the venue smells of chlorine and Ben Gay. What is needed are sheer volumes of accessibility…pooltime. The community pool at the retirement village is the primary opportunity to build friendships. Think about that for a moment. The majority of our time that we spend "in church" is often confined to services. Services are composed of one person leading some singing and one person speaking. Your church might have some variance on that formula…but it's more a matter of numbers than it is format. Suffice it to say, the majority of our time is spent observing or perhaps participating in singing, but little time is allotted for the building of relationships. Here at the cement pond today, exercise is really just an added benefit to the environment. I'm just here on vacation, but even in my temporary circumstances I can pick out the regulars. They greet each other as they walk through the gate. They inquire about family and show interest in health updates. This is a place where interaction takes place and where invitations are shared. This is a place where followers of Christ have an opportunity to be church, not just do church. Someone is going to lose a spouse…and in that moment when the Spirit of God, who does the bidding (not our job), actually has their attention, they're going to search for hope in the lives of anyone committed to them. Somewhere in that moment, they're going to think of their new found friend and the hope that is evident in their friend's life. That's incredible and equally troubling news.

It's troubling because it implies that if their greatest connection is to a secular resource or perhaps a cult…that is where they are going to turn. Have you observed such phenomena? Americans today simply want to know what works. They're not choosing religion based on theology or doctrinal stance…they're making choices on perceptions of success. If it works…sign me up.

So is the American church working? Those outside the church, which constitute the majority of people in America, would answer unequivocally "no". Is there any hope for change in the church if people within the church believe all is well while those outside the church cannot understand why we do the things that we do?

A buddy of mine is fond of saying, "The church spends great amounts of time answering questions that no one is asking." Great thought, but here's an even greater one…why is that?

Where are the fish in your neighborhood and what questions or thoughts have they?

Sometimes an illustration can be taken too far. Sorry.

Is your church positioned at the edge of perceived stream? Remember when we were consumed with the placement of our church buildings? Did it have good exposure? Was there room for expansion? Were we close to new neighborhoods being built?

Having one's building sit next to a highway with an off ramp near was a great advantage back in the day. You could build a new building and people would come Sunday morning simply out of curiosity. One of the mega-churches in my neighborhood is building a multi-million dollar expansion right now. It's huge…it will be first class…it will compliment the youth center…and I'm convinced that most people really do not care.

I'm certain that a year from now…after all of the hype is over…that it will be just another big building in town. I fear for any church that hires the entire ministry done…that builds buildings in order to attract more people…and that relies on cutting edge ad campaigns to build a crowd. I fear for them because it bypasses the body of Christ and does not convey that the development of the spiritual gifts in it's members is absolutely necessary for the full expression of the church to be realized in the community. I fear for them because that model of evangelism and community impact will not be sustainable. When leaders adopt such a philosophy, what message do they send the next generation of church leadership? Good luck finding the quarter of million dollars necessary to get the next attractional church plant off of the ground.

If it's no longer possible to launch ministries with such external polish evident that outsiders take notice, where do we begin to find fish and how do we engage them? They're at the YMCA soccer field…they're at the PTA…they're in the cub scout den or the girl scout…den, pack…I'm not certain what girl scouts call their gatherings. The fish are on either side of your house. On my block, they are at the Christmas cookies exchange or the neighborhood garage sale. They are found hovering around anything landscape oriented. They're there...you just have to look.

The fish are in places that the church...especially the suburban church...is not willing to go. They are in poor neighborhoods. They're in urban areas that the church abandoned years ago. They are in apartment complexes and trailer courts. They are in nursing homes. They are parents of handicapped children...who are scared to death of taking their child to a church knowing the possibility of their child disrupting the events of the morning.

Jesus said the harvest is plentiful...or, as I like to translate it...the pond is stocked. It's time to employ the depth finder. It's time to find out where the fish are and go after the fish...regardless of whether they are the type of fish that you would like to fish for. I've said it before...when fishing...one of the things you want is quantity....numbers....LOTS O' FISH. In the next chapter, I'm going to talk a bit about who the fish are. It's one thing to see the cement pond in a new light. It's another thing to know who the fish are in the water. If we care about the fish, we'll take time to listen. Listening to fish...now there's a peculiar picture.

Chapter Six: **Slimy Worms**

What appeals to me may not be the best bait.

I'm sitting on the tile floor of O'Hare International waiting for a plane. I like the sound of that…it sounds so "writerish". I only fly a couple of times a year…I'm certainly no jet setter. I've chosen the tile floor with a pillar as a back support because I'm in need of a bit of space. Lots of people…very little room.

From my vantage point, one thought repeatedly comes to mind. Everybody's different.

They walk different….dress different…smell different. At least that can be said for the guy in the white cap who just passed me. Here's a fun little thing to do next time you have two and a half hours to kill between flights. Try and find someone wearing the same shirt.   My shirt of choice today…an orange, long sleeve number. Certainly the manufacturer of my wardrobe choice produced a gazillion of these shirts, why is it so rare to find someone wearing the same thing as you?

If there is one commonality it's that we're not all that common. Diversity…that's what I see around me. God's creation…whether they know it or not. Mere observation demands the question, how can one appeal or one approach…one worm, if you will, catch such a great diversity of fish, I mean, people?

What's the correct approach to reaching the gentleman who now passes…earring, long fuzzy hair, white t-shirt, brown shorts…tennis shoes and no socks, truly a Ted Nugent want-to-be. How does "orange dress shirt guy" connect with "T-shirt, no socks guy"? Let's consider the lady with short gray hair, sweat pants and flowered top now passing by or the Indian couple…or the kid with the bandana…or the member of the "grumpy miners" softball team. What bait will they bite on?

There are many who come from church traditions that believe the proclamation of God's Word…the preaching of truth…will in and of itself draw a crowd. It's the "preach it and they will come" philosophy. There are others that prescribe that "orange dress shirt" guy should never even attempt to connect with "T-shirt, no socks" guy. To do so, in their minds, would be a colossal waste of time.

I wish there was a universal solution to catching fish. Some might say the secret resides in the fish…that the fish have to be hungry enough to take the bait. While that's true in the fishing world, I'm not sure it's always true in the case of humankind. I wish it was easy. The optimist in me longs for a simple approach. My prior training, perhaps primarily subliminal in application and content, taught me to preach and let God sort em out.

By the way…the guy with the "grumpy miners" shirt just walked by again…good looking shirt. I would wear it.

Paul states in 1 Cor 9: 19-23, "Though I am free and belong to no man, I make myself a slave to everyone, to win as many as possible. 20To the Jews I became like a Jew, to win the Jews. To those under the law I became like one under the law (though I myself am not under the law), so as to win those under the law. 21To those not having the law I became like one not having the law (though I am not free from God's law but am under Christ's law), so as to win those not having the law. 22To the weak I became weak, to win the weak. I have become all things to all men so that by all possible means I might save some. 23I do all this for the sake of the gospel, that I may share in its blessings." For Paul, maturity was placing others before self. Doing so was not a program or a ploy. It was a display of cultural sensitivity to the degree that his personal comfort level took a back seat to the need to connect and relate to the person across the table. Did you hear that?

He changed in order that others might change, and…he went first. He did not gauge the potential response of his audience and then weigh his options. He changed in order that he might win "some".

Is that the perception people have of American Christiandom today? I think not. Let me suggest that instead of changing in order to connect or respond to an increasingly pluralistic culture, most people see Christians as immovable, dialogue resistant people. Why is that? I'll propose one possible answer. I think we're intimidated.

We're not near as certain about the truth of God at work in our lives and in the lives of others as we like to externally maintain. I believe we're apprehensive that if we enter into a dialogue with people of varying beliefs and philosophies, we might make a mistake or reveal our ignorance. Some of us are afraid that other systems of belief might make equal sense, or at a minimum require the same level of faith that we place in Christ. Some consider such conversations as "casting pearls before swine", which all too easily alleviates us of any need for connection. Please understand that I'm not slamming the individual. Whatever the reason, I place the vast majority of blame on a system that placed the truth of scripture solely in the hands of the Theologian or professional clergy. The man, or woman, on the platform possessed revelations from God that those in attendance were incapable of discovering on their own. True enough, when the majority of society was illiterate, having someone who could open the scrolls and read the things of God was a necessity, even a blessing. However, most of our American culture is literate. Furthermore, for the reader of English, the Bible has been translated in so many ways that keeping up with new translations and paraphrases is a job unto itself. I was in a bookstore this past week and saw a Bible translated into comic book form. The broad strokes of scripture were graphically illustrated along with the necessary "Pows" and "Umph" that all good action comic strips contain. I might have to get a couple of those for my two teenagers. Then again, I might just have to get one for me.

Why do we feel the need to defend Jesus? Do we believe if we make a mistake or are incapable of answering a question concerning scripture that we will in some way diminish the power and authority of Christ? If the Gospels teach us anything, and they certainly teach us a lot, it is that the people who followed Christ…the Disciples or students at Christ U…had moments of revelation and glory, and many more times of ignorance and a lack of execution. However, God CHOSE them.

I believe it was that choosing that gave them the necessary confidence. They came to see themselves as Christ's ambassadors. It was through the realization of a new identity in Christ that the New Testament church would adapt and change and become effective in telling others about Christ. Meeting physical needs was not simply meeting physical needs. It was done so out of a new identity the church had in representation of Christ. Up until now I'd not given it much thought, but surely there had to be people in the infancy of the church who were reluctant on some aspects of relational connection and were almost giddy about others. Some broke bread with earnest, others broke bread because they understood it to be beneficial to the cause. Some sold property and gave with glad hearts. Others were reluctant to give but gave just the same. The story of Ananias and Saphira comes to mind, not because of their reluctance, but because of the condition of their heart and ultimately their lack of identity in Christ. They were carried and buried not because they were reluctant to give, but because their reluctance was greater than their love for Christ.

Their reluctance literally took their lives.

This chapter proposes that what we use as bait may not be the thing that is most effective. We may prefer to use an artificial lure because it doesn't wiggle while we place it on the hook, but what we prefer may not be what entices the fish. Thus the question…when is fishing more about the fisherman and when is it more about the fish?

If the days of inviting people to attend a Christmas musical or Easter cantata as our primary means of evangelism or connection with the community are no longer effective, do we get to continue with that lure and hope that the fish change their mind? I remember those days. I've always been sort of a ham and have participated in a number of church plays. They were a lot of fun, and usually…the church was packed out. People came to see the set. They enjoyed the music. For the most part, it was a great time. But inevitably, after the play was over and the holidays had passed…the church had not grown in attendance. The fish had either slipped off of the hook, never took the bait, or belonged to another aquarium. Being a guy who appreciates the creative, if I had my way, we would do nothing but concentrate our efforts in making the Gospel and the Church more attractive.

I dig theater lights and new music. I like humor and appreciate a creative example. There's nothing wrong with those things…UNLESS…they constitute the sole effort in reaching lost people. In other words, if the fish don't bite on your favorite lure, you don't have the right to refuse to change.

So what is the best bait? I'm glad you asked. We'll talk about it in the next two chapters.

Chapter Seven: **Picky Fishermen**

In the previous chapter we discussed whether you and I get to choose the bait with which we are most comfortable, regardless of whether or not the fish are biting on that lure. In this chapter, I want to discuss whether we get to choose the fish that we go after.

Perhaps this is where the illustrative commitment of this book breaks down, for fishermen usually know for what they are fishing. I've heard the occasional surprise statement upon reeling in a catch at the end of a line, "Well, would you look at that??", but for the most part what lies at the bottom of the lake is pretty predictable.

People aren't nearly as predictable.

Over the past couple of decades, the American Church has been greatly influenced by evangelism campaigns that encouraged leaders to target specific populations, much in an effort to reduce the unpredictability factor. Targeting involved creating church services that spoke the language of certain populations, communicating through examples and illustrations generated from that populations' lifestyle, and relaying spiritual truth through culturally relevant art and music. Someone told us we needed to get creative. Somewhere along the line we found it necessary to jazz up what was considered a bland and culturally irrelevant message.

If I were talking about a missionary effort to an unreached population on the other side of our globe, most of what I just stated would be highly regarded by churched folk. We readily accept that missionaries in foreign countries have an obligation to learn the language, customs, and cultural expressions of the people to which they desire to minister. There are many who would go so far as to offer that the missionary must utilize cultural icons to communicate a spiritual message, that Paul himself provides an example by referencing the "unknown God of the men of Athens". Many would agree that the goal, after all, is not to Westernize people. The goal, rather, is to communicate the significance of the gospel. A quick story comes to mind. Let's talk about that significance just a moment.

This past week we had a mission's event at our church. Nothing awe-inspiring about the event. We simply opened up the building, brought in some great homemade desserts, and listened to a presentation…all in just under two hours. The missionary to whom we listened credited his start in missions to the place in which he stood and noted that he had responded to a call to mission 35 years earlier. Three and a half decades in ministry is amazing enough. Three and a half decades of translating the Bible into a language that has never been written down is another thing all together. The man who stood before us had spent over half of his life developing a written language for a Hispanic tribe of 4,000 people known as the Huarijio. After developing a written language, and actually creating new words for concepts and objects unknown to the Huarijio people, he was close to having translated the entirety of our scriptures.

Consider such effort for a group of people less than the attendance of the mega-church around the corner from me. Consider again such effort when every possibility exists that the people for which the text was created may not pick it up and read it.

The missionary had laser like focus. He knew who he was fishing for and knew exactly what bait was necessary. We think about focused efforts in foreign missions like the previous example and commend the intentionality that is so foundational to the work. The question remains, Can we lead the church in America with the same intentionality? Do we angle for specific fish? Do we possess the enduring tenacity displayed in the example of our missionary brother?

My thinking on the topic has moved some 540 degrees, if that's possible. I've moved from believing that targeting demographics in ministry was a necessity, to believing that targeting demographics belittled the role of the Holy Spirit, to once again believing that knowing who we are fishing for is necessary. So I've been around this "target fish" loop one and a half times. Who is to say whether I'll make it a complete 720?

Unlike the popular notion that America is a melting pot, I see greater independence and commitment to unique cultural expressions than ever before. Perhaps the internet has played a big role in drawing people groups together or perhaps it's more possible than ever to be independent in our lifestyles. Whatever the reason may be, I rarely see the necessity to conform to a common lifestyle. That's not to say that we don't have common elements that the majority of us experience. My wife and I have always laughed over the common occurrence of a Bed, Bath, and Beyond located next to Office Max which is located next to Hobby Lobby. If you even know one of those stores, it speaks to how common the everyday American experience can be. Could it be the corporatization of America that drives us to retain unique independent expressions?

In an age of hundreds of channels of cable television featuring everything from history and cooking and sports and news and weather and comedy and science fiction and I could go on and on, do we have an option to provide a one stop spiritual shopping experience for the American consumer? I don't see how. I'm not commenting on the universality of the sacrifice that Christ made for all of humankind or undermining the Lord's broad appeal of forgiveness. I am commenting on the greatest diversity of individual mental processing that America has ever known. Increasingly, we think different today.

While I believe that more targeted approaches in ministry are more necessary than ever before, I want to caution the American Church in three areas. I believe a continued consideration of these areas will help us avoid some pitfalls currently experienced in extreme definitions of what it means to be the church in America today. Those three areas are:

1. Exclusion: The problem with fishing for specific fish is the fish that are left behind. While they may not prefer the bait being offered, the truth is that they occasionally bite. The fisherman is pleasantly surprised upon reeling in something that he didn't see coming. If people don't fit a demographic, but choose to participate, the church must do it's best to make them feel a part of the collective. That doesn't mean that they need to switch bait. To do so is simply to leave a different category of fish behind. That's not an answer.

In America, all should be welcome in our churches, but all will not fit…which leads to another conclusion. The kingdom of God has many fishermen. Assumption that others will fish for the ones that we leave behind is not good enough. Our aim is to fish the pond empty of fish.

2. Maturity: Writing that "all may not fit" makes me a bit nervous. It's one of those unwritten statements that any ministry leader who has led more than two years quickly realizes. It makes me a bit nervous, not because I'm uncertain in what I'm saying, but due to my lack of control over the perception of those who read those words. For a new follower of Christ to read that some people will not fit in certain expressions of the American Church is a difficult concept to understand. Often, the new believer needs the church to

be perfect, and we…the church attenders…easily recognize that need and choose a mask over transparency. The other person who struggles with that statement is the immature believer. These folks may have attended church for years, but lack the motivation or see the necessity to understand the culture around them in order to process the ministry efforts of the church. Both groups carry an emotional toll on people around them. There are highs experienced in the innocent questions of the new believer and there are lows associated with the murmurs and complaints of those who wish we could return to days of the past.

I propose that we must partner with the new believer and address their misconceptions about church and church life and find ways for continually removing any pretense of perfection in the life of its members. Furthermore, we must define what maturity looks like for the long-time follower of Christ. Without some handoff, holding hands will continue to be required.

3. Witness: Inclusion of fish that don't fit the requirements for which you are fishing is a witness of the power of God to those around us. For that reason alone, I caution the Church in allowing the concept of targeting to be associated with isolation. I was recently in a church plant in downtown Los Angeles that was specifically targeting two demographics that most would not place in the same sentence…high rise condo owners and street people. The church was located two blocks from Skid Row and nestled among renovated business buildings turned yuppie condo. As intriguing as

was the combination of these two people groups, what I found more fascinating was the church leadership's commitment to balancing the effort to reach the groups. 70% attendance of condo dwellers yielded the necessary funds to bring in 30% street people. The leadership went so far as to say that an increase of street people led to a decrease in condo dwellers with the condo dwellers perception that the church was becoming a "homeless church".

I conclude this chapter with that recent experience for a couple of reasons. One…it's possible to include fish that we never intended to catch and two…fishing in America isn't easy. But just like Tom Hanks said of baseball in "League of Their Own", it isn't supposed to be easy. "It's what makes it hard that makes it great."

Chapter Eight: **Where the fish are**

Perhaps it's a little weird to include a chapter on where to find fish. Though I'm no professional angler, I'll go out on a ledge here and state as a matter of fact…fish are found in water. They occasionally jump out of that water, but only to confound the previous statement and prove once again that God has a sense of humor. SUCCESSFUL fish, however, return to that water. In general, fish lying on a river bank are not in good shape. Fish were created for water, and it's in the water that they most naturally develop.

SO…for the fisher of men, it's just a matter of finding the water. Fair enough?

I came across a book in the fishing section of our local library entitled, "The Big One". This book by David Kinney details his experience upon entering a fishing contest on the island of Martha's Vineyard. The author spent 35 days in quest of a great fish. I've not completed the book, so the jury is out on whether he accomplished his goal. The jacket of the book makes an interesting statement on Mr. Kinney's motivation. It states, "While he currently ranks among the 90 percent of fishermen who catch 10 percent of the fish, he's working to change that." I'm not sure I could sum up the intent of this book in any more precise or greater fashion.

Let's return to the idea of an island based fishing tournament. The Kinney book contains pictures of dozens of fishermen casting lines in the water from the beaches of pricey accommodations. No matter which way one wanders on the island, eventually one runs out of real estate. The island is precisely an island because it is surrounded by water, and in this case, is center to the activity at hand. The islander has no doubt where the fish are.

Now a question for consideration. Is the American Church positioned in the midst of the water, or have we moved inland to avoid potential storms? Inland sounds safer, doesn't it? We don't worry much about hurricane season in Indiana.

Positioning is a big deal. I've said it before, but it bears repeating. The problem with Christianity in America is not one of relevance; it is a problem of accessibility. "But we have a church on every corner, how can you say that?" I agree we have numerous church buildings, many of which are very empty on Sunday mornings. I agree that we have many programs and that we pray that God would send revival to America. I'm not anti-building or against programs or prayer initiatives, however, I don't believe that adding more of what is already not working effectively will yield a different result.

The problem is accessibility. People who need Christ don't know someone who has Christ. Furthermore, people who have Christ don't speak up anymore. I'm not talking about argument here or a campaign for Christian rights or even the legislation of morality. All of that has been tried and the results are less than stellar and perhaps a contributing factor to our present condition. I am talking about people developing the ability to engage in a spiritual conversation without the need to get defensive or embarrassed. I'm talking about verbalizing what God has been doing internally in our lives…and if He's not been conducting himself in a manner that you understand…admitting that our actions and beliefs often require the execution of faith. Lately I've been thinking about how ashamed we are made to be of the concept of faith. What's wrong with faith?

While I don't believe that the church remains in the mainstream of American society any longer, I'm not one to relegate us to the farm fields of my native Hoosier state. Instead, I believe we've taken more of coastal residence. We've got an ocean view. Perhaps we're located across the street from the beach. Perhaps that street is very busy and, in the end, we expect the people to leave the water and risk life and limb in order to reach us. Perhaps we're just a respite from the heat or something else.

John Candy rented a beach house in the movie Summer Rental. Since it was located next to the board walk, people kept asking to use the bathroom or get a drink of water. Eventually the house was full of beach goers utilizing the amenities of the house.

It would be nice if we could simply open the doors and people entered with obvious needs that could be met. I believe there are two challenges with associating this illustration with the church. One, the needs of Americans are not overtly obvious. There are major issues of poverty, education, and health care…but those issues are so "major" that the local expression of the church often has no idea where to begin in addressing them. Further, there may be no motivation to address needs due to our reliance on government systems. "That is, after all, why we pay taxes" comprising common reasoning. The second issue plays directly off of that last consideration. The church located on the beach suffers from a lack of public awareness. Many Americans no longer associate the Church with answers to life's challenges and problems. The local bookstore has shelves full of self-help books. The public turns to the internet to find out what someone they've never met has to say about their problem or issue. They turn to government programs, they listen to talk radio, and they return to school. They do practically everything possible before thinking of the church.

We're located across the street from the beach, but no one pays much attention.

If that's a little overwhelming I'm about to give you some great news. It's time for you and me to go to the beach. If the beach goers won't come to us, it's necessary that we cross the street and go to them. We must enter the water. Let's talk about jumping in.

There was a time I would have defined the water in terms of the church soccer league or the Christmas musical. I was a firm believer that the church should offer every attractional program possible in order to win some. Basketball leagues and support groups…scrap booking parties and scouting dens…If it was legal, moral, and did not run contrary to the principles of scripture, I was all for it. I guess in some ways, I still am for those things…but not for the same reason.

Originally I saw them as methods of evangelism. They were relationship building methods for the purpose of evangelism. Over the past few years I've come to see several problems with this approach. One, the relationships that were built often lacked any possibility of leading beyond a superficial engagement. Two, when the activity was concluded…often the relationship lacked enough benefit to continue beyond the scheduled time. I don't believe this is an indictment on particular activities…for I believe that participating in most church services on Sunday morning carries the same relational constraints. I'm certainly not against the assembling of the church for worship and teaching, but if we believe that relational connections are being formed strictly through that one activity, I believe we're fooling ourselves.

I don't believe that the water in which we are to wade is comprised of church softball leagues or revival services. The water that you and I are called to engage is the human condition itself. Softball and other activities might be the vehicles that get us there, but they fall far short of reaching the depths in which real transformation is possible.

David Kinney, in the aforementioned book, details a time that he spent with a tournament participant in his 35 day fishing venture on

Martha's Vineyard. He asked the professional angler how long he should wait before attempting to reel in a trophy winning Bass...three seconds...five seconds? "It depends on the fish", was the answer. The professional went on to explain that most fishermen fish in superficial ways...their focus lying on top of the water. Instead, the professional envisions the bait below the surface moving among the rocks and the crevices. In the pursuit of many fish, the real fishermen know you have to fish the bottom.

But the bottom is messy...and so is life.

So where are the fish? They're in the water...on the bottom...and it's Christ's mission to reach them where they reside. Consider this thought for a moment. Can you recall a time when people encountered Christ without need in their life? Perhaps the rich, young guy who Jesus instructs to sell his possessions and follow him...perhaps he didn't display an obvious need, certainly not one of desperation. But for the most part, people who searched for and found Jesus often did so because they had a need in their life. Their kid was sick, they were the scum of society, or they were guilty of sin. Consider for a moment those who believed they were beyond any need...much less a need for Christ. Consider the Pharisees. If there is a self-righteous, self-fulfilled group of people that get on Christ's nerves, it's those who in religious terms cannot recognize the filth of the rags they wear.

Jesus met people at their point of need. Many times that meeting resulted in physical needs being met, but without a doubt Jesus demonstrates a greater priority than the feeding of the masses or causing the blind to see. Upon encountering a lame man lowered through the roof of a packed house, Jesus first forgives the man of his sins. Healing his non-functional legs was a blessing to the man and a witness to those in attendance, but the most loving thing that Christ could do was to open the door to eternal life. That, indeed, is the most loving thing that you and I can do as well.

So…the Softball team might open the door to a conversation about a marriage relationship heading for the rocks. A scrap booking club may yield a dialogue about addictive behaviors. A talk across the fence may plunge beyond the surface to reveal uncertainty about the future. Question…if we were to allow others to plunge the depths of our lives, would they find the same challenges but filtered through a Biblical worldview?

God's church can no longer afford fishing on the surface. We cannot equate participation in an event with spiritual depth. Put on your waders…it's time to get closer to the fish.

Chapter Nine: **When We Become The Bait**

We've all had times when we felt like a worm. This chapter will propose that worm may be exactly the role you and I are to play. Such thoughts always remind me of bumper stickers, and the absolute absurdity that such a bumper sticker would portray. "Follow me to Acme Church. We're a bunch of worms"…probably not the best marketing campaign.

Lest you think that I'm associating the follower of Christ with a misguided sense of humility or possibly a life that lacks a good self-image, let me emphatically state that nothing could be further from the truth. While I'm not a purveyor of a prosperity doctrine, I am hard pressed to understand how our heavenly father does not take pride in rewarding obedience in addition to bearing the emotional toil of punishing our disobedience. Jesus explained it this way, "If you then, though you are evil, know how to give good gifts to your children, how much more will your Father in heaven give the Holy Spirit to those who ask him!" (Luke 11:13)

Doesn't it make sense that God would take care of his children? Scripture is replete with examples of how people demonstrated need and how God responded with supply. We, however, do not serve God simply for what he might give us. God is no heavenly Santa Claus. I propose that much of our problem with an American expression of Christianity is that we have sold Christianity as just that, a means to get more out of life, to get a better life. The question is worth consideration, in what ways is it a better life to serve Christ?

Put down the book for a moment and consider the question yourself. How has your relationship with God changed your life?

Wouldn't it be great if all of the people in our churches could articulate a response to that question? My guess is that most of our people would struggle to respond. Many were raised in church going families. Many are second and third generation products of Christianity. As with the duplication of a copy that was duplicated that was duplicated that was duplicated, there's a bit of dulling that accompanies the duplication process. Perhaps the awkward silence that purveys the room in response to that question speaks of that duplication. Heading my own advice, but in this case taking time to walk away from the keyboard, I believe my answer to the question can be boiled down to three primary statements.

(1) The greatest way in which my life as a follower of Christ is better is in my understanding of the state of my soul. (2) Closely related to that is the belief that what I see around me is not the full expression or extent of reality…I will live forever with God. And (3) I don't have to do this life on my own. I have extended family through the work of Christ that is dedicated to walking with me through life as I am equally committed to them.

Those things make my life better with Christ as opposed to a life without him. Have I lived outside of Christ…certainly, we all have. Have I experimented with other expressions of religion or investigated other philosophies of life? "Experimented" might be too strong of a word. "Investigated" would certainly apply. I have probably learned as much about my belief system through observation as through formal methods. Observation is a powerful tool. It can be good and bad…often at the very same time.

For many in our culture, observation is the largest obstacle to crossing a line of faith, for their observation is not on the eternal, but on an expression of our values in the here and now. They see the house in which I live. They observe my relationship with my children. They evaluate the number of complaints I register. They watch how I work. And it's not just me that they observe…anyone claiming a Christian moniker is valid. They note the news when it speaks of religious leaders abusing their power. They listen to how people treat each other in the church. They listen to our evaluations of good versus bad sermons, preferable music over a differing style. They observe how we spend our money, or for the money for which we beg. They listen when we can't agree on the most important thing of all, Christ himself.

They are much more savvy than we give them credit for.

Ultimately, they evaluate whether followers of Christ display a sacrifice like the Savior in which they serve. Michael Frost in his book "Exiles" states, "We have imprisoned (Christ) in a stained-glass cell and want only to worship him, never to follow him."

What does it mean to follow Christ? My simple answer is that it means that you and I become the worm. We are the bait, and being the bait is not necessarily a pleasant adventure.

I'm about to venture into a "preachy" mode. My goal is not to impress, but to persuade. We've all been impressed by many things in our culture. Far fewer times have those impressions led to a compulsion to engage. Furthermore, my intention is not to condemn, but to spark some conviction. Conviction is a good thing. Conviction means that we're still sensitive enough to feel. Knowing scripture is far more than memorizing sentences or understanding the historical context. Conviction, as well as the warm fuzzies that accompany obedience, is a result of knowing the authors voice…not just a matter of crossing "I's" and dotting "T's".

The jury is out on whether we can once again focus on scripture that instigates heart felt conviction. Perhaps there's never been a more necessary time than now for us to examine such scripture.

Jesus did not shy away from the controversial. Knowing the sacrifice he would make permitted him to ask for complete allegiance to his mission. Jesus asks the crowd to consider the cost of following him when he states in Luke 14: 25-35, "If anyone comes to me and does not hate father and mother, wife and children, brothers and sisters—yes, even their own life—such a person cannot be my disciple. [27] And whoever does not carry their cross and follow me cannot be my disciple." Was he really implying that Christians hate those who stand against them in their faith? To view this passage simply as a shock jock statement is to miss the point of Christ's message. Jesus goes on to say that it would be foolish to begin to build a structure without calculating the entire cost for the project. The goal of the project is completion just as the goal of following Christ is sharing in his mission and in the blessing of obedience. Is there a real cost in following Christ? Jesus wants everyone to know that allegiance to him may even cause division within the strongest societal bond of that day…the institution of family. Jesus unashamedly requires priority one.

In Matthew 10 he sets the scene for what the Disciples can expect to experience in the proclamation of their faith. "I am sending you out like sheep among wolves." (Mt 10:16) As if the reference to potential, many would say probable, family conflict wasn't enough, consider the scene that combines wolves and sheep…have you seen what wolves do to sheep? But instead of bunkering down and hiding from the world, Christ's encouragement is to value what is pure and be as sly as a serpent.

And the hits just keep on coming…

Jesus instructs the disciples on the blessing of their connection to him in light of a combative environment in which they are called to minister. John 15: 18-20 "If you find the godless world is hating you, remember it got its start hating me. If you lived on the world's terms, the world would love you as one of its own. But since I picked you to live on God's terms and no longer on the world's terms, the world is going to hate you. In 2 Tim 3: 20 he reminds them,"Servants don't get better treatment than their masters."

Just ask Paul how his life, in physical expression, got better after his blinding encounter with Jesus. Paul tells the Romans, "We also glory in our sufferings, because we know that suffering produces perseverance; [4] perseverance, character; and character, hope." (Romans 5: 3-4) Paul sees purpose as well as process by hanging at the end of the hook. He demonstrates definite "worm mentality" when he tells the Corinthians, "We have this treasure in jars of clay to show that this all-surpassing power is from God and not from us. [8] We are hard pressed on every side, but not crushed; perplexed, but not in despair; [9] persecuted, but not abandoned; struck down, but not destroyed. [10] We always carry around in our body the death of Jesus, so that the life of Jesus may also be revealed in our body. [11] For we who are alive are always being given over to death for Jesus' sake, so that his life may also be revealed in our mortal body." (2 Cor 4: 7-11)

While I don't seek trials or problems, Paul teaches that it is through the circumstances of life that God will reveal his power, glory, and provision. Does that imply that God cannot work through "thick" as well as "thin"? Absolutely not, but one must consider the power of our testimony. When is his power most evident…in times of self-sufficiency or in times of personal weakness?

So, in my interpretation and for your consideration, life is found "on the hook". Losing our lives for his sake is the only way to find real life. Living as bait is largely dependent on the work that God does on the inside of my life.

Remember. Somebody's watching.

Chapter Ten: Equal Opportunity Aquatics

I don't watch a lot of movies, primarily because most of the movies I've seen in the past decade have left me longing for a refund. That might seem a reasonable statement if I were willing to pay the $10 admission required at most theaters. It's an especially revealing personal statement considering that my movie expenditures primarily consist of dollar theaters and Red Box rentals.

Adopting this approach for all things pop culture requires a bit of patience. As I see it, given enough time the movie that I'm ever so slightly interested in will eventually make its way to television. Do I subscribe to the movie channels? And here, I thought you knew me better by now.

So my eldest and I were watching basic cable the other night when "The Perfect Storm" happened across the screen. I found myself slightly interested. Prior to all of the intense action of the storm, the fisherman are fully engaged in their mission of commercial sword fishing. They bait hooks and sink lines deep in the water in their search for a great catch.

The scene that inspired this diatribe occurs when they begin to reel in one of the fishing lines. As they work to bring their catch to the deck of the boat the captain comments that whatever the catch might be, it was certainly a large one. Just at that moment, a great white shark leaps from the water and attempts to swallow Mark Wahlberg.

The star of the moment…the fish…makes one primary mistake. Everyone knows you never go after the lead actor too early in the film…a supporting actor, that's a different possibility. Regardless of the mistake, the impact of the sudden lunge to the deck of the boat produced the shock and awe so desired by the director.

Consider some other examples of fishing surprises. Forest Gump's initial efforts came up empty handed in his search for shrimp. If memory serves correct, he caught a toilet seat and a rubber boot. Chevy Chase caught a snake while fishing in "Funny Farm" and after becoming entangled with the fishing line was so scared by his catch that he spent the next couple of scenes trying to outrun the snake he drug behind him. If one is interested, a quick Google search for "great Hollywood fishing scenes" yields a quarter of a million hits. I took a look at the first one and then lost interest after that.

What does interest me is how unpredictable fishing efforts for the follower of Christ can be. With all of our efforts to offer the appropriate bait to catch a particular fish, one cannot know what will work or what is destined to fail once the bait sinks into murky waters.

Ananias knew firsthand the uncertainty of the catch. He is told in a dream that he is to go place his hands upon a murderer and confirm the call of God upon the killer's life. Oh…and the target of the mad man's anger is people just like Ananias. (see Acts 9)

Ananias objects to the murkiness of the water. Ananias would have related well with Mark Wahlberg. Saul was nothing less than a Great White shark.

Jonah was the same way. Having received specific instructions concerning a God ordained fishing expedition, Jonah decides he doesn't like the fish he's told to pursue. Once again, the fish in this case are enemies of the fisherman. In great demonstration of God's humor and appreciation for irony, Jonah the fisherman becomes Jonah the bait. For three days, the fish wins.

Ultimately, Jonah gives in and fishes for the Ninevites. Ultimately, he tells God what he claims to have known all along…Jonah claims he could see into the murky depths and by doing so, really doesn't learn anything personally or allow God to be God. Jonah saw the Ninevites as Carp. Perhaps it's not too much of a stretch to assume that he was afraid of them as well.

I don't want to equate all non-believers with Selachimorpha and Cyprinus Carpio; that would be unfair. I don't want to imply that fear is a natural product of fishing for the unknown. Indeed, the fishing experience should be one that's rather natural to our lifestyle, certainly not a production or a chore. I do want to make the case that one can never be certain of what they will catch.

A number of years ago I took a group of college kids to Brooklyn, NY to work with inner-city kids. These college kids went into the high rise projects and visited with children who attended the many activities of the church. When not in direct contact with the kids, those same college kids stocked food pantry shelves and painted school buses. Upon returning to Indianapolis, a fishing question rose from our ministry debrief.

If they could fish for kids in Brooklyn through the many methods experienced over the past week, why couldn't we fish for kids in Indianapolis? One question led to another...if feeding people was an effective method of building relationships with others, why don't we feed some people? If taking Sunday School out of the church building and performing it on the sidewalk was more effective than what we were doing inside the building, why don't we take it outside?

All were good questions and ones that deserved answers.

Those college students took it upon themselves to begin with what they had and fish for others. They gave themselves away in the process. They became the bait. They visited kids in their homes. They prepared lessons but more importantly participated along with the children. They fished and trusted God for the catch. One of the kids who got caught up in the passion of these students was a little boy named George.

An African-American inner-city kid, George had virtually nothing in common with the white suburbanite college kids from the mega-church. What George did share with the workers of the Backyard Bible Club was common heart. Authenticity speaks volumes, even to a kid.

Now 20 years later, the Backyard Bible Club has grown into an inner-city church with significant connection in the lives of that same neighborhood. George is on staff and serves as youth pastor. People are fed, shelter is provided, and addictions are addressed. All because a bunch of college kids went on a fishing trip to Brooklyn, NY and caught a bug for fishing.

Jesus shared a parable about a man who had a great feast prepared for his guest. However, when it came time for his guests to attend the banquet, they all had excuses for why they could not attend. The master of the banquet ordered his servants to go into the streets and bring in total strangers. There would be no pedigree honored, the invitation was open to all.

Salmon or Bass, Walleye or Trout, Swordfish or Great White…all fish…and people…matter to God.

Chapter Eleven: **When the Fish Aren't Biting**

I had a bit of a theological melt down the other day. It was more melt down than theological, meaning that it was much more me than God. It was very purposeful, however. I remember thinking in the middle of my rant that I, indeed, had choices to make as the words left my mouth. I could take safe passage, or I could tread a path more laden with risk. I was in a mood…so the path of jagged stones and unpredictable turns seemed more appropriate at the time. I'm not certain that it was more profitable.

The scene was in a Lutheran church of which one of the very best pastors I know presides as primary man behind the pulpit. Around the room were 5 other pastors of varying denominational backgrounds. For the past year and half I had spent time with this sorted bunch of ministers. The topic, of which we were to each respond, consisted of three questions. One, how have we been doing since our last meeting? Two, what were our expectations for the group? And Three, on what do we believe the group should focus in the next 18 months?

It was a "lay your cards on the table" sort of meeting. We had spent some time together as a group…even done some traveling together…but we now faced a growing tension among the members that needed to be addressed. My Lutheran buddy excels at pointing out the unacknowledged elephant in the room. His ability to do so had brought us to a crossroads.

When it came time for me to discuss the three questions, I started out all right. Answering where we were as a church wasn't all that different from what other guys had communicated in the room. Like others, our congregation attendance was down…finances were down…and we were weathering the storm. The guys in that room had seen storms before and they had seen God bring them through. In hindsight, I can say that none of the circumstances of the moment led to my preaching to the preachers. My diatribe began with the second question.

What were my expectations?

I've spent the last three years studying the idea of mission and movement in America. I've encountered a number of people who believe that multiplication movements do not exist in our country. That's a bold statement, and one that is as difficult to prove, just as is the counterpart…that movements do exist. Is the Tea Party a movement? Is Facebook a movement? Is same sex marriage a movement? Is the ALS Ice Bucket Challenge a movement or a mere fad? What constitutes a movement?

If defining a movement isn't challenging enough, let's further complicate the matter by focusing on a further qualification. What is a multiplication movement? Earlier in the book I referenced a statement often heard, "It's worth it all if only one person gets saved." Does one person constitute multiplication? I'm not making a statement on the worth of one individual. I am asking if addition is multiplication?

Outside of family relationships in an American context, how many of the lives of followers of Christ contain a multiplication factor? Allow me to explain that a bit. How many of us have stories of two or three people that we have participated with in their pursuit of Christ who in turn have engaged with two or three people in their pursuit of Christ? I'm no mathematician, but if I had three people I was discipling who in turn had three people each, that's a group of 13 people. If 75 people in a small church employed such a system that small church would reach 975 people in three generations of the process.

My diatribe really took shape when I expressed that I'm no longer interested in hearing that multiplication movements within Christianity do not exist in America. I've seen the numbers. I understand a lack of motivation in the traditional church as well as a misplaced enthusiasm in the contemporary one. I struggle with a lack of power and confidence like others do and I fear for my children and their understanding of God as demonstrated in the American church. All of that said, I don't want to hear anymore about what we're not...especially if you're not willing to put any skin in the game. Let's talk about who we are. Let's utilize what we possess instead of lamenting our lack. Let's talk about what we truly can be and not just what we long to be.

A friend of mine recently started ministry in India. Talking with him on Skype the other day, I learned that he has 70 people to baptize who have accepted Christ as Savior. When I asked him how this had happened, he told me that he had not sent out a flyer or began an organized outreach of any sort. He told me it started by leading one person to Christ…and they in turn went home and told their family what Christ had done for them. The family then invites my friend to come and talk about Jesus, and more people get saved…who tell others.

That's multiplication. I'm excited for my friend, and a bit jealous. It's the way that evangelism and the multiplication of lives are intended to work. And while I'm excited about the blessing of God on my friend's efforts, I am a bit skeptical. First generation Christians are excited. First generation Christians often experience miracles. First generation Christians aren't worried about having just the right words to say. Second, Third, and Fourth generations…that's a different story.

And while it's a different story, relegating the move of the Spirit of God to historical trends is something that I'm not willing to do. Perhaps God wants to do a first generation work in the heart of a fourth generation believer? Would it be permissible to believe for such?

Which leads me to the challenge of this chapter…what do we do when the fish aren't biting? I'll offer four things for your consideration.

One: We don't give up. Taking the line out of the water will assure that we catch nothing. Blaming the fish won't get more fish on the line. Comforting ourselves over our lousy catch won't make us more successful our next time out. Wishing that conditions were different and lamenting on and on about how great the fishing was in days gone by won't change the circumstances…so let's stop complaining.

Two: God promises us a catch. He didn't tell us to pray for the fish, he told us to pray for the fishermen. Let's take God at his word.

Three: If one fishing hole doesn't work, try another. I've included the location of numerous fishing holes in the appendix of this book.

Four: Our lives are the bait that either attracts or repels the fish…there's no two ways about that. Scripture tells us that if we will lift up the name of Christ, HE will draw all of mankind unto himself. (John 12:32) I interpret in the following manner. If Christ's transformational power is alive and well in me, then those around me who desire transformational power will be open to the call of God. Is it really more complicated than that?

It's the simplicity of that statement that makes this perhaps the most difficult chapter to compose. Why is it we blame the institution of the church for the ineffectiveness of our individual lives? My answer is because we delegated the responsibility of the individual to conglomerate. If we sang the right music or focused on the "relevant" passages of scripture, people would invite others to church. And if the church was full, certainly we were doing something right? Participation, or at least observation with enough attendance, could be interpreted as transformed lives, couldn't it?

How do we measure whether a Sunday morning, attractional activity commonly referred to as "church" in America OR a missional, individualist embodiment of the incarnate power of Christ is effective in producing the kind of lasting change we so desire? Answering that question within the unique context which God has placed you is imperative in a culture with increased distraction and alternatives.

In summary… we won't see a different result unless we embrace the individual responsibility of being representatives of Christ. Unless we begin to see our lives as living examples of Jesus 24 & 7, we will continue with the same mediocrity that we currently experience. I heard somebody say "we must put flesh on the gospel". I believe that was Christ's intent all along. Paul said it best, "I no longer live. It's Christ living in me." (Gal 2:20)

Lastly, unless we have some process of measuring and holding the church accountable for the mandate of living as Christ before a lost world, this book and any talk of this subject will be just another organized group of papers upon the shelf.

Chapter Twelve: **Catch and Release**

I've never written a book before, numerous articles and papers for school, but never a book. What I've discovered in this process, which I engaged sporadically over the past four years, is how the material I thought I would present for consideration developed with a new focus never intended at the outset of this effort. That's a development that I did not see coming and one that intrigues me and scares me all at the same time. My conclusion is simply this…I have changed as the material has changed. More specifically, my observations, expectations, and thoughts on application have changed. I am hoping that you've changed a bit in your position as well.

When I began this work, the thrust of this chapter was the need for churches to release people in ministry…to trust the recent catch with the heart of the gospel…to intentionally release transformed fish back into the waters to influence other fish. "Hey, getting caught isn't so bad. There really is life beyond these waters", summating the encouragements of the recently hooked.   Too often the recently caught are only presented opportunities for ministry within the walls of the church. You can be an Usher fish…or an Alto Fish…or a Youth Sponsor Fish (the craziest fish of all). However, if you want to be a Single Mother Guppy who reaches like Guppies, there may not be room for that in the church.

I still believe that churches need to release people in ministry. The failure to do so has dire consequences of which I believe we are beginning to see in the attitudes of 20-somethings today. There are many people who see the church in America as an institution without a cause. Ask those same people about Habitat for Humanity or the Red Cross and they willingly open their wallets in support of those efforts. I'm not knocking Habitat or the Red Cross. I am wondering how sheltering people and taking care of the downtrodden became an effort outside the realm of the Church? Didn't Jesus say something about true religion and its focus on widows, orphans, prisoners, and the hungry? While I was born in "Good Samaritan Hospital" in Vincennes, Indiana, I've never attended "Good Samaritan Church". In fact, most of my observation of missions in church has focused on the construction of church buildings or Bible schools, I don't recall many wells dug for clean water. I have observed medical missions efforts when a group of doctors, dentists, or nurses could be assembled in the church. Such efforts were often relegated to more secular efforts and, while it was never vocalized, were deemed less spiritual in nature.

Allow me to offer a hypothetical story on how I believe many para-churches got their start. By para-church, I'm referring to ministries that exist beyond the walls of First Church. Remember the Single Mother Guppy who reaches other Guppies reference? Let's expand a bit on that example.

Single Mother Guppy takes the bait of a like Guppy and discovers a power for her fish existence that she has never previously known. It's only natural for her to share her experience with other Guppies. Pretty soon, a whole school of Single Mom Guppies, both hooked and non-hooked, are meeting together and discussing life beyond the murky water and in the murky water. With every explanation of the benefits of being hooked, New Christian Single Mom Guppy is energized. With every day that passes by, she grows spiritually deeper and increasingly bold in word and deed.

One day it occurs to her that perhaps the church could help in her passion to encounter other like Guppies. She approaches Pastor Bass who listens to her enthusiastic, but inexperienced explanations for the vision she has for other fish in the pond.

To her dismay, Pastor Bass explains a number of disillusioning problems. One, she hasn't been hooked long enough. Only fish that have been hooked for an extended period of time are qualified to influence other fish. Two, other fish like her won't really fit the school of fish that reside in the aquarium. Three, since most of the ministry in the aquarium and the budget required for that ministry is focused on aquarium fish, there really isn't any budget for exploring different waters. Finally, with every indication that new fish caught would not feel comfortable with the fish in the aquarium, why would Pastor Bass support such a fishing expedition? The not so subtle implication is that the only fish truly worth hooking are the ones who join the local school of fish on Sunday morning.

New Christian Single Mom Guppy walks away dejected…but quietly determined. She recalls the excitement of her new life beyond the murky pond, so she decides to begin her fishing expedition anyway. Because it's not sanctioned by Pastor Bass, recruitment for her efforts must be covert. In this story, fish talk…and some of the most talkative fish one can find reside in Pastor Bass' aquarium. Eventually, all of the aquarium fish know what Guppy mom is up to. She's a believer, but she's a rebel. She is familiar with the waters of the aquarium, but her school of influence resides in another group of fish all together.

Do you see the problem? Because Pastor Bass has no kingdom mindset or apostolic values, ministry must be limited to what is within his control. If it doesn't happen in the aquarium, there's no room for it. Instead of building upon the passions of the increasing numbers of fish, all energy is given to assimilating them into life in the aquarium. Instead of trusting and listening to the prompt of the Holy Spirit in the lives of believers, or fish in this case, greater faith is placed in leadership training and strategic planning.

And that's where this chapter took a turn that I had not anticipated at the outset of this book.

I'm the first to say that I enjoy, and believe in, the task of leadership development. I think and function much better with words and thoughts composed on a page. I often develop teaching plans several months in advance and engage leaders in assessing church culture.

As much as I employ those things, I do not believe that they can replace the necessity of the Holy Spirit's lead in determining the next steps for the church.

Perhaps there are two reasons why strategic planning and leader development has taken priority over a Holy Spirit dependent entrepreneurial arm of the church. First, allowing the Spirit to lead is scary for some and too messy for others. It's easier to default to controlling efforts and micro managing details. Secondly, it's possible that we do not fully embrace the peculiar identity and unique nature of the church.

When it comes to releasing fish in order to reach other fish, are we confident in what we're inviting newly hooked fish to join? The story offered suggests in humorous portrayal what I believe are serious problems. If every fish hooked is only truly hooked when they join your church, that's a real problem. Jesus didn't tell us to fish in order to build larger fish sanctuaries. His life, which focused on transformation and the message of the kingdom, resulted in the greatest vessel ever designed for catching and releasing fish…the church. There's nothing greater than the assembly of Spirit drenched followers of Christ gathered for the express purpose of sharing their faith and fulfilling the Great Commission.

You've experienced that, right? Is that how you would describe your church?

Author Reggie McNeal states that one of the greatest paradigm shifts we must face in the western church is a switch from seeing our mission through the eyes of the church to seeing the church through the eyes of mission. Until we do so, I'm not convinced that many of us have ministries worthy of new fish acquisition.

Kingdom ministry embraces all fish even when doing so stretches others in the school.

Conclusion: **Everybody Oughta Fish**

There's an old joke about an elderly gentleman who goes fishing with the local game warden. The two are in a boat in the middle of a lake when one guy pulls out a stick of dynamite, lights it and throw it in the water. The dynamite blows up and several fish rise to the surface. The game warden is aghast. He states, "You can't fish like that…its illegal!" The old guy just takes out another stick of dynamite, lights it, and hands it to the warden as he inquires, "Are you gonna sit there, or are you gonna fish?"

Sometimes I wonder whether fishing for men is all about the finesse of bait and lures…or whether it's better simply to throw another stick of dynamite into the water just to shake things up a bit.

When Jesus touched the lepers, he lit a stick of dynamite. When he engaged the woman at the well, he lit another stick. When he ate in the home of the tax collector, when he defended the woman caught in adultery, and when he forgave the sins of a lame man…boom, Boom, BOOM.

There's a time and place for every type of fishing, and it would be amiss to suggest that one model should take precedent over another. Holding that line in the water for a family member may take great patience and endurance and be the exact method required for success. Equally valid is the technique of fishing the dangerous waters of the Bearing Sea in consideration of the challenge of missions in historically spiritually dark places.

Regardless of the context, we are all called to fish. We're called to murky waters, to offer our lives as bait, and believe God for the catch. Though we may be tired, we are called to launch out into new efforts at the leading of Christ and fish 10' to the left. And when God brings in the catch, we're called to release people into ministry with the firm belief that God will use them to reach those in schools of fish that you and I may never know.

None of that obligation should be relegated to task only. To be called by God to engage the world around us is privilege. To engage in the promised certainty and invigorating experience of landing a great catch is to operate within our purpose. To fish on, and ultimately be caught as well, is the goal.

> The Fisherman's Prayer
> I pray that I may live to fish, until my dying day.
> And when it comes to my last cast, I then most humbly pray:
> When in the Lord's great landing net And peacefully asleep
> That in His mercy I be judged
> Big enough to keep.

I wish you nothing but success on the lakeshore.

Fishing Holes in America

1. Support groups
2. Bowing leagues
3. PTA
4. Auto enthusiasts club
5. Bridge club
6. Neighborhood Association
7. Summer Concert volunteer
8. DIYers
9. Pet clubs
10. Little League
11. Book clubs
12. Food Pantry
13. Alumni Association
14. Band Boosters
15. Kiwanis and Rotary
16. Health club
17. Flower society
18. RVers
19. Motorcycle club
20. Fraternities/Sororities
21. Scrapbookers
22. Facebook/Pinterest
23. Business associations
24. Coffee shop
25. Classroom
26. Scout troupe
27. Drama Group
28. Local café
29. Homeless shelter
30. Barbershop / Beauty Salon
31. Neighborhood pool
32. Social Justice groups
33. Emergency response groups
34. Veterans groups
35. Hospital ministry
36. Homebound Boomers
37. Investment/Finance groups
38. Ecology Group
39. YMCA programs
40. Show Choir Volunteer
41. FFA
42. Hotel travelers at Christmas
43. Juvenal Court System
44. Childcare ministry
45. Homeschoolers
46. Firefighters, Policemen, Soldiers
47. Summer day camps
48. Funeral needs/grief support
49. Holiday Blockparty
50. The neighbor across the fence.

About the Author

Though not an avid fisherman himself, Chet Berry owns three fishing poles of varying condition and quality as well as one inherited tackle box. The tackle box is somewhere in the attic and the fishing poles are hanging from the house rafters in an entangled mess.

Chet is a graduate of Indiana University and holds Masters degrees from Fuller Theological Seminary and Saint Mary of the Woods College. Chet serves as lead pastor of Hope The Breakfast Church.

Chet is married to his wonderful wife Marchelle. The Berry's have three children, two dogs, and one gerbil. In his spare time Chet likes to play guitar, wash the family Jeeps, and lament over the condition of Indiana University basketball.

Contact: chetberry@yahoo.com